1,2&3 John

Dwell in Light

Sarah K. Howley

Flaming Dove Press

Flaming Dove Press
an imprint of
InspiritEncourage LLC
1520 Belle View Blvd #5081
Alexandria, VA 22307
www.inspiritencourage.com

ISBN 978-1-960793-42-3 (e-pub)
ISBN 978-1-960793-43-0 (paperback)
ISBN 978-1-960793-44-7 (large print)

Printed in the United States of America

Library of Congress Control Number: 2025927132

Contents

Welcome

to this Study of 1,2&3 John

These three letters are attributed to John, the same author associated with the Gospel of John and the book of Revelation. Though the first letter did not specify its audience, many scholars believe it was intended for believers throughout Asia Minor, in what is now modern-day Turkey. These were likely among the last of the epistles written, dating to the late first century, around 100 AD.

John had been exiled for preaching the gospel of Jesus Christ and for refusing to worship the emperor of Rome. It was during this time that he wrote Revelation. These letters are believed to have been written following his release from exile and return to Ephesus.

John wrote the letters to strengthen and instruct the church in the truth of the Gospel. The tone is very pastoral. He encouraged believers to remain steadfast in faith and obedience. He assured them of eternal life through Jesus Christ. The second and third letters continued in this manner, addressing faithfulness, hospitality, and discernment in the Christian community. Together, these letters called believers to dwell in the light of God

– holding to truth, walking in love, and living with confidence in Christ.

Each session opens with introductory questions, followed by a reading from one of the letters of John and questions related to the passage. Then the session turns to linked Old Testament passages for comparison, expansion, and reflection. Each session concludes with personal application questions. Additional tips and suggestions for approaching the study individually or in a group follow.

Suggestions for this Study

This study is designed for individual or small group study and is composed of 8 sessions from the letters of 1, 2, and 3 John. It is designed to encourage thought and discussion of the scripture, encouraging individuals and groups seeking God to have conversations about the text. For 'You will seek me and find me when you seek me with all your heart,' as Jeremiah 29:13 says.

General Guidelines for Individual Study

1. Open each session with prayer. Ask God to speak through his Word.

2. Respond to the introductory questions that focus on the theme of the session and what God says in the main reading.

3. Read the passage more than once, perhaps in different translations. Using different translations can offer expanded viewpoints on the meaning of the original text. This study uses the New International Version (NIV) as the basis of questions

and quotes. However, any version may be used to provide insight and assist in revealing meaning.

4. This study is designed to offer a starting point for discovery of what God has to say to you through his Word. Because the study looks at how the Old Testament is reflected in the epistles, there are observation and interpretation questions about the readings in John's letters and then about the links in the Old Testament, as well as comparisons between the passages. These are followed by application questions for personal reflection and group discussion. Writing your responses will provide clarity and focus your thoughts on the verses.

5. Use a Bible dictionary or other reference books to look up any unfamiliar words, places, or names.

General Guidelines for Group Study

1. Come to sessions prepared. Some groups will choose to read and respond ahead of time then gather and discuss together; others will gather to read and discuss together. Before beginning, agree how you would like to proceed so all are prepared.

2. Be an active participant in the group by sharing your thoughts and responses to the questions. Groups often have members who are in different places in their walk with Christ and each perspective should be valued.

3. Listen to each other. Consider the amount of time that is available for all to share and be careful not to dominate the conversation.

4. Be open-minded. Participants are encouraged to be open to learning and sharing, even expecting alternate viewpoints. The Bible serves as the foundation of this study and hearing other perspectives may challenge your own understanding. When differing views arise, the focus should remain on listening to each other and encouraging one another to wrestle with difficult passages and concepts rather than building consensus.

5. Maintain group confidentiality. For participants to be willing to share and grow, the trust level in the group must be high. Do not share what is shared in the group outside of the group unless permission is given to do so.

6. Expect God to meet you in the study. His Word is living and active (Heb. 4:12) and he is present when we gather in his name (Matt. 18:20).

Introduction

When you think of "light" and "darkness," what qualities or emotions come to mind?

Why do you think truth and discernment matter so much in faith?

Session 1: God is Light

1 John 1:1–2:6

Opening

Many churches invite the congregation and visitors to a time of "fellowship" after the service and some host "fellowship" meals or potlucks. How would you define fellowship and what makes it meaningful?

Confessing when we are wrong can be difficult, whether privately or publicly. Why do you think acknowledging our faults feels challenging?

As John opened his letter, he began with what he had personally seen and heard of Jesus, inviting believers into the fellowship that comes from knowing Him. He introduced the theme of God as light, a picture that shapes how believers understand truth, sin, and life with God. These verses lay the foundation for John's call to walk in the light with honesty and trust. This opening sets the direction for the themes John develops throughout the letter.

Read 1 John 1:1-2:6.

Reading Questions

What did John say gave him authority to write this letter?

What contributes to the believers' joy, as referenced in John 1:4?

List characteristics of living in spiritual light and contrast those to living in spiritual darkness (1 John 1:5-10).

Describe the advocate in 1 John 2.

How can we be sure that we know Jesus Christ?

Summarize how John says believers should live.

Old Testament Link

John's description of God as light reflected a deep-rooted theme of the Old Testament. The psalms particularly described God's light as central to His character and relationship with people. Confession and forgiveness were also vital parts of Israel's active life with God. These passages provide a fuller understanding of these ideas.

Read Psalm 27:1 and 36.9. How is light portrayed in these verses? What do these descriptions add to our understanding of God as light?

Read Psalm 32:1-5 and 51:1-10. How do these passages illustrate the process of forgiveness. Together with 1 John 1:9, outline the steps or pattern you note.

Application

Take a moment to reflect on something you have not brought before God in confession. Write a prayer acknowledging it and seeking his will.

John ended this session's passage saying that those who know Christ will walk as He did. What areas of your life most reflect His example and which areas reflect Him less clearly?

Session 2: Unchanging Commandment

1 John 2:7-17

Opening

How would you describe "worldly" things and how would you describe "spiritual" things?

What helps love endure over time, whether a love found in friendship, for family, or for a stranger?

John's letter continued with a reminder of the command of love, old instruction renewed for the Christian life. John's call for Christlike behavior and love carried fresh meaning for those living in challenging times. John contrasted love for God and that for the world and its desires. He called on love, maturity and communal life to shape how the believers lived out their faith.

Read 1 John 2:7-17.

Reading Questions

Summarize this "old command" that John gave those who read the letter.

Who did John write this letter to according to 1 John 2:12-14?

List at least three reasons John gave for writing to the church. Which are repeated?

What did John indicate the world consisted of?

How did the world impact the life of the believer, according to John?

Old Testament Link

The contrast of love for others and love for the world in this section reflected long-standing laws from the Scriptures. Israel was called to live set apart from surrounding nations, showing love for both neighbor and foreigner while remaining holy to God. This separation, or holiness, was reinforced by John in the passages for this session.

Read Leviticus 19:17-18 and 19:34. How was love described in this verse? What expectations or limitations were put on the Israelites in these commands?

Read Leviticus 11:44-47 and 20:26. What reason did God give for them to be holy? What did being God's possession mean for Israel? How does this compare with John's call to love God rather than the world?

Application

Loving one another can be one of the most difficult commands in Scripture. How do you demonstrate God's love to everyone, even those who are difficult to love?

Holiness means being set apart for God's purpose. John outlined how believers were to live apart from the world and for God's purpose. How do you see the connection between holiness and love expressed in your own life?

Session 3: Children of God

1 John 2:28-3:10

Opening

Consider a church, a football team, a club, or a family. What gives people a sense of identity and belonging?

At times, it can be difficult to distinguish between right and wrong. What are the benefits or challenges of clarity in moral issues?

In this passage, John encouraged believers by reminding them they are God's children, set apart through relationship with him. He contrasted righteousness and truth with sin and deception, contrasting those who follow God with those who belong to the world. Believers were reminded that their identity and behavior revealed who they served and reflected either the character of God or the influence of the world. Living as children of God meant dwelling in His light – reflecting His truth and love in daily life.

Read 1 John 2:28-3:10.

Reading Questions

How did John say God demonstrated his love to believers?

Note how John contrasted the righteous and the worldly in the chart.

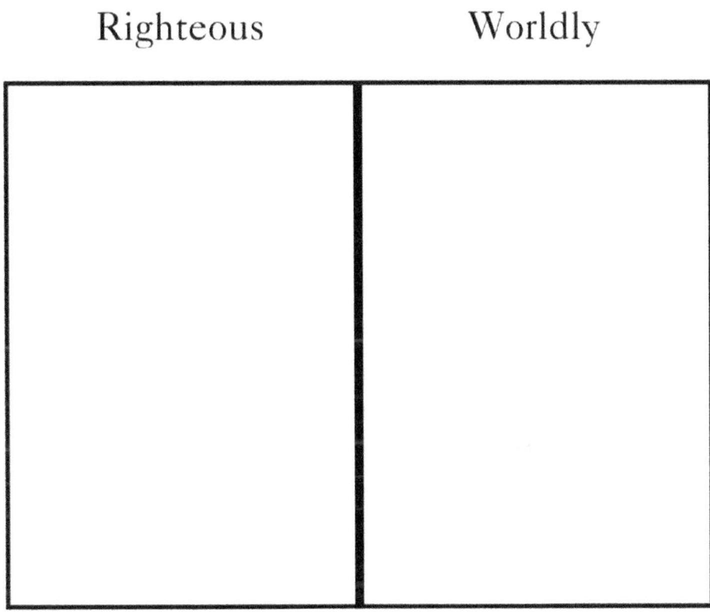

What reason did John give for the Son of God appearing?

What was the result of being born of God?

Old Testament Links

In this passage, John wrote of how believers' identity and behavior were shaped. These themes were central in the Old Testament as well. Israel was called to live holy and righteous lives and was also described as children of God. John's emphasis on these themes revealed the importance of right relationship with God.

Read Deuteronomy 30:8-14, Psalm 119:9-16, and Jeremiah 31:32-33. How do these passages describe living without sin or remaining faithful to God's commands?

Read Deuteronomy 7:6-9, 8:5, 14:1-2, and Hosea 11:1. In these verses, God referred to Israel as his child. How does God's love for the people of Israel compare with the love shown to believers in 1 John 2:28-3:10?

Application

Though forgiveness is not specifically mentioned, John referred to it when speaking of the need for purifying and leaning on Jesus to take away our sins (1 John 3:3-5). Take a moment to confess your sins to God and ask him to purify your heart.

According to John, righteous actions reflect God's character and our relationship with Him. What are three things you have done recently that revealed his influence on your actions or choices?

Session 4: Love One Another

1 John 3:11–4:6

Opening

Have you ever lost your way, even when using a map? How did you get back on track?

What makes a test reliable? How do you decide when something, or someone, has passed or failed?

John continued his use of contrasts, turning in this portion of his letter to themes of love and hate. He described love as evidence of truth, and a mark of spiritual discernment and direction. He challenged believers to test teachings and look for evidence of

God's presence in others to discern what is true and what is false. By recalling the greatness of God, John encouraged believers to stand confident before Him.

Read 1 John 3:11–4:6.

Reading Questions

What is the evidence of God in believers?

How did John describe or define love in 1 John 3:16?

What commands ended 1 John chapter 3?

How do we know God is in us?

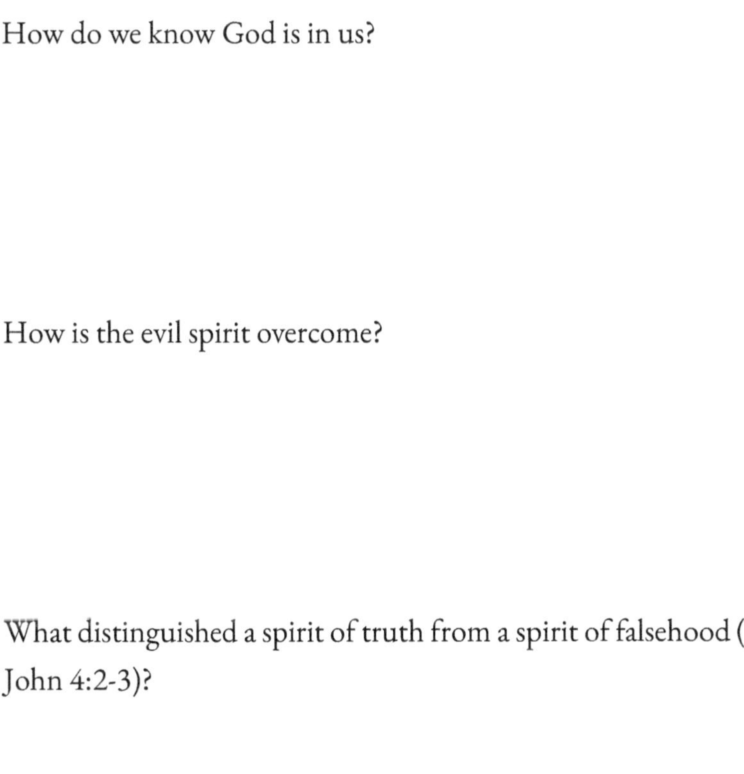

How is the evil spirit overcome?

What distinguished a spirit of truth from a spirit of falsehood (1 John 4:2-3)?

Old Testament Links

John wrote that the "one who is in you is greater than the one who is in the world," reflecting the ongoing conflict between God's Spirit and false or evil spirits found in the Scriptures. The Old Testament accounts illustrated these opposing forces and showed God's authority in discernment, offering evidence of this strength for believers in John's time.

Read 2 Kings 6:15-17 and 2 Chronicles 32:6-8. How do these accounts of God's greatness and the strength of his army expand the understanding of John's statement in 1 John 4:4?

Read Isaiah 44:24-26 and Ezekiel 13:1-9. How do these passages differ from the instructions John gave regarding testing the spirits? In what ways were John's readers better equipped for discernment than the people of the Old Testament?

Application

Believers rarely have an opportunity to literally lay down their lives for another. What are some daily examples of how this love can be expressed? How have you experienced this love from others in your own life?

When have you faced circumstances that seemed bigger than your faith? How does remembering that God's Spirit within you is greater than any circumstances you face change the way you see those situations?

Session 5: Love Made Complete
1 John 4:7-5:5

Opening

How do people usually describe what love is and how it grows?

How does fear influence people's decisions?

John interwove the themes of love and life throughout this letter, returning to them again in this section. He wrote of love as the identifying mark of God's children and described its expression through obedience, and its power to overcome. John connected faith, love and victory showing how they shaped the lives of who followed Christ.

Read 1 John 4:7–5:5.

Reading Questions

What is the source of love and how is love given to one another?

In what ways did God show love?

Why did God give his Spirit to believers?

How is love made complete?

How were fear and love related according to John?

What command was given about love?

How is love for the children of God demonstrated?

What is the key to victory?

Old Testament Links

God's love and his victories were refrains of joy throughout
the Old Testament. The descriptions of love expressed

through obedience and how faith overcomes adversity were long-standing patterns in Scripture. The exhortations to love others and the accounts of triumph through trust in God's power illustrated how faith and love worked together in the lives of God's people.

Read Deuteronomy 6:1-6 and 10:12-15. In what ways do these verses show love and obedience working together? How does this deepen understanding of 1 John 5:2-4?

Read 1 Samuel 17:45-53 and Psalm 20. How do these victories that came through trust in God, help illuminate John's description of overcoming the world by faith?

Application

Remember that the heart's attitude matters as much as the action itself. The opposite of obedience is not only disobedience or rebellion; it can also be reluctance or resentment in carrying out what is asked. Which of God's commands do you find most challenging to follow? What stands in the way of obeying with joy or peace?

John wrote that perfect, or complete, love drives out fear. What situations most often bring up fear in your life, and how could God's love help you respond with confidence?

Session 6: Belief in the Son
1 John 5:6-21

Opening

A sense of safety or security is one of the basic needs of human life. What makes people feel protected or guarded from harm?

Why is it easy to become distracted or drawn away from what we value most? What helps people keep faithful to their commitments?

As John moved toward the end of his letter, he returned to the theme of assurance for those who belong to God. By highlighting the Spirit's testimony about the Son and the gift of eternal life, he invited believers to rest in the certainty of their relationship with God. This confidence shaped how they approached prayer and understood God's protection, reminding them of their secure position as His children.

Read 1 John 5:6-21.

Reading Questions

How did Jesus Christ come and how can we be certain of this truth?

What has God's testimony given believers?

What do 1 John 5:12-13 assure the believer?

What was the purpose of John's letter?

What topics did John urge believers to pray about?

For what purpose had God given understanding?

Old Testament Links

John's assurance of life in Christ echoed long-standing themes in the Old Testament, where God chose His people, sustained them, and promised life through His faithful presence. These passages reveal how life with God was grounded not in human certainty but in God's character and commitment. They offer deeper insight into the confidence John described for those who belong to God.

Read Deuteronomy 7:6–9 and 14:1-2. How do these passages describe God's choosing of His people? What aspects of God's character in this text deepen understanding of John's assurance that believers "may know" they have eternal life?

Read Deuteronomy 30:19-20 and Psalm 36:7–9. How is life portrayed in these passages? What connections can you make between this description of life with God and John's statements that "life is in His Son"?

Read Isaiah 55:10-11 and Jeremiah 32:38–41. What promises does God make to His people in this passage? How might these promises shape a believer's confidence in belonging to God, as described in 1 John 5:18–20?

Application

John wrote that his readers may know they have eternal life. How does knowing you belong to God influence the way you face uncertainty, temptation and fear?

What most competes for your attention or loyalty? What tends to guide your actions? How can you remain certain you are carrying out God's commands in the face of distractions and competing priorities?

Session 7: Love in Truth

2 John 1-13

Opening

There is much discussion today about fake images and false stories in the media or on social media. What helps people recognize when something is true?

What is the difference between receiving a reward that has been earned and feeling entitled to one?

John's short second letter addressed several themes that greatly influenced believers' lives. Addressed to the "chosen lady and her children," it charged them to live by truth, to demonstrate love in action, and to discern truth. John also warned against those who distorted the truth and urged them to remain steadfast in their beliefs.

Read 2 John 1-13.

Reading Questions

Of what command did John remind this letter's readers?

How did he define love in 2 John 6?

What was John's warning to the recipients of the letter?

What lesson did John want teachers to deliver to help in discerning the truth?

What would make John's joy complete?

Who sent greetings along with John?

Old Testament Links

John's call to live in love and to guard against deceptive practices echoed familiar refrains from the Old Testament. God's people were given commands to guide relationships with Him and with others. False prophets appeared throughout Israel's history, and they were warned to remain faithful rather than be deceived. These passages highlight how John's message reflected enduring teachings of God's word.

Read Exodus 20:1-17. From these well-known commands, which speak about relationship with God and which about relationship with others? How does the single command to love one another encompass the spirit of these commands?

Read Deuteronomy 13:1-5, 18:21-22, and Jeremiah 23:16-17. How were false prophets described in these passages and how did they present themselves to the people? How do these verses reinforce John's warning about deceivers?

Application

Which people in your life can be challenging to love? Choose one of God's commands and consider how you could put it into practice toward them as a demonstration of love.

John encouraged faithfulness to God in anticipation of a full reward. How might love and discernment of truth shape your attitude toward that promise, rather than a sense of entitlement or expectation?

Session 8: Faithfulness & Fellowship

3 John 1-14

Opening

What qualities define a leader? What happens when these qualities are not present in a leader?

What purpose does hospitality serve within a community or organization?

In this, the shortest book of the Bible, John encouraged his friends to remain steadfast in faith and to live with love and truth. He acknowledged that some in the church acted wrongly and commended those who continued to do what was good. John also noted the importance of fellowship among believers and anticipated resolution through proper authority.

Read 3 John 1-14.

Reading Questions

Summarize the opening greeting of the letter.

How do hosts share in the work of the missionaries?

What were three problems that John identified in the church? Who was the leader of this?

What advice did John offer Gaius?

How could Gaius understand who to trust?

Why did John write so little to his friend?

Old Testament Links

Though John does not reference any verses in the Old Testament directly, the patterns of hospitality, integrity and leadership are rooted there. Integrity of character and hosting others were consistently demonstrated through accounts of individuals in Scripture. They continue to mark God's influence in others in John's time, as ours.

Read Genesis 39:1-12, 1 Samuel 12:1-5, and Proverbs 9:8-11, 11:1-3. What do these passages reveal of integrity and faithfulness? What characteristics might Gaius have sought in support from others in his trials?

Read Genesis 18:1-8 1 Kings 17:8-16, and 2 Kings 4:8-10. What kind of relationship existed between the host and guest in the accounts? Why were the hosts eager to offer hospitality? What parallel can be seen between these examples and Gaius' actions in 3 John?

Application

It can be challenging to continue doing what is right when others, especially leaders, do not. What helps you stay steadfast in your actions?

John contrasted faithful and self-serving behavior. How do these behaviors impact how someone's reputation is viewed? What qualities would you like others to see in your character and conduct? Do you need to work on or add these qualities?

Conclusion

John's letters emphasized truth, love, and faithfulness as defining marks of those who belong to God. He reminded his fellow brothers and sisters that faith was seen as obedience, love expressed through action, and discerning what is true. In the three short epistles, John encouraged confidence in Christ, cautioned against deception, and highlighted integrity and hospitality within a community of believers. These writings revealed the character of a life shaped by fellowship with God, guided by His truth and love.

How have these three letters most changed or deepened your understanding of what it means to "dwell in light"?

How might John's description of a faithful life, one marked by obedience, love, and integrity, guide your relationships and choices moving forward?

What did you learn about God from this study?

What did you learn about yourself from this study?

Do you believe that Jesus is the Messiah, the Son of God and have you received life in his name? If so, describe the qualities of that life.

If this is the first time that you have answered yes to the call of following Jesus, please reach out to a local church or the author to share of your choice and find support for your new life.

To continue your deep dive into "Seeing the Old Testament in the Epistles", pick up *Romans: Trust the Faithful God* to continue your study. Find it at your nearest retailer by scanning the QR code today.

Romans:
Trust
the
Faithful
God

Also By Sarah K. Howley

Seeing the Old Testament in the Epistles
Ephesians: Experience God's Power
James: Know God's Wisdom
1&2 Thessalonians: Prepare for Christ's Return
Hebrews: Elevate Jesus
Philippians: Pursue Christ's Joy
1&2 Peter: Grow in Grace
Revelation: Worship the Lamb
Colossians & Philemon: Live Transformed
1,2&3 John: Dwell in Light
Romans: Trust the Faithful God

The Son Reveals the Father
I Am: An 8-Session Study of John
Heart: A 12-Session Study of Luke
Word: An 11-Session Study of Matthew
King: An 8-Session Study of Mark
Our Trustworthy God: How Much God loves You, Joyfully
Engages with You, and Trusts You

Women of the Old Testament Bible Studies
Hope: A Bible Study of Women in Jesus' Lineage
Faith (coming 2026)
Love (coming 2026)

Alive Again Bible Study on Forgiveness
Alive Again: Find Healing in in Forgiveness
Alive Again Bible Study: Find Healing in Forgiveness
Alive Again Forgiveness Prayer Journal

About the Author

Author and founder of InspiritEncourage, Sarah K. Howley writes Bible studies that reveal the transforming depth of Scripture and lead readers into a thriving relationship with God. Known for weaving Old and New Testament connections with warmth and insight, she invites believers to encounter God's truth in everyday life. She fuels her writing with espresso—and gratitude for any gluten-free/dairy-free dessert she didn't bake herself. Sarah and her husband support global initiatives for literacy and hunger relief.

You can find Sarah on Facebook and Instagram @inspiritencourage. To book Sarah as a speaker at your next event, please contact her through her website. For weekly encouragement and information on her latest releases, sign up for Sarah's newsletter at InspiritEncourage.com.

InspiritEncourage